18 MOMENTS OF POETRY

D. W. MAPPS

---

18 MOMENTS OF POETRY

Vanguard Press

VANGUARD PAPERBACK

A CIP catalogue record for this title is
available from the British Library.

ISBN 978 1 80016 175 7

*Vanguard Press is an imprint of
Pegasus Elliot MacKenzie Publishers Ltd.*
www. pegasuspublishers. com

First Published in 2021

**Vanguard Press
Sheraton House Castle Park
Cambridge England**

Printed & Bound in Great Britain

Dedication

To my wife, Trudy Creswen Mapps

Acknowledgements

I would like to express my gratitude to my granddaughter, Olivia Mapps, whose help in compiling this book to present to the publisher was invaluable. To my dearest sister, Moreen Lewis, and my brother, Morris Mapps, thank you both so much for your encouragement. A special thank you to Pegasus Elliot Mackenzie for all your help and understanding to make this book come into existence. Finally, thank you to my wife, Trudy, who had so much faith in me.

Contents

Introduction

My name is Derrick William Mapps. I was born in a place called Llanbradach near Caerphilly, South Wales in the UK. My father's name is Henry and my mother's is Margaret. My dearest sister is Moreen and my brothers are Graham, Morris and Wayne. Like all families, they all find a path to go down, and my path eventually led me to Cwmbran. I married a wonderful woman called Janet and over the years we had five children, Amanda, Derrick, Stuart, Gary and Sharon.

Sadly, as life is, when everything seems to be going well heartache comes, and it did on the 18th of August 2000. Janet died of M.N.D. That's when things in my life went a little bit strange, which you will read in the chapters.

Then, on the last Tuesday in April 2006, I met a woman called Trudy who so encouraged me. She would always say, "You have been given a talent, and you must use it or lose it, and I won't let you do that." You will also meet her in the chapters. Say hello from me when you do.

Anyway, the reason I am talking to you is this book. I have been given an amazing gift of poetry. Yet, out of all my poems, *The Tree of Dreams* is the only one that is a book. Over the years I have been saying I am going write a book on it. I know all the characters off by heart; they have been calling out for nineteen years. And writing this book, *Eighteen Moments of Poetry*, has given me the confidence to go ahead with that project. I can't wait to introduce you to it. It's a very magical place. Also, to my friend, Michael Read, a farmer from Abergavenny, thank you. As you navigate through the chapters, I hope some will make you smile, or perhaps cry in joy on your journey.

Thank you.

D. W. Mapps

Moments

Every journey starts with a step. Well, my story started with a word. It was just over six months after my wife, Janet Elizabeth, had died in 2000. I was walking through the town centre in a place called Cwmbran when I encountered my late wife's auntie. She asked me how I was doing, the same question everybody seemed to ask.

"I am all right," was my reply. Then I added a comment. "I heard her voice last night."

"You did?" she asked.

"Yes," I said.

Then she replied, "If you hear them call your name they're telling you that they are fine and not to worry."

With that, I said, "It was nice to meet you." I said thank you, then left.

In the night, getting ready to go to bed, I heard my name called. I went to the bedroom window, and looked out: two white sheets were on the line in the garden. I was thinking someone was hiding behind one of them. I knew my wife's voice. I was actually thinking she was out there. Then the wind blew, the sheets moved. No one there. I got into bed thinking I was going crazy. I fell asleep.

This was when it went crazy. I was dreaming. I found myself in a beautiful meadow, a stunning place; it felt so peaceful. Then I saw my wife raking grass in this meadow. "Janet," I called.

She turned towards me and said, "I am all right," and told me to go.

"Come with me."

"No," she said. "You must go."

Just then a white light so bright was standing next to me. I just knew it was someone.

"You must go now." A voice spoke out to me.

Just then I woke up, thinking that was so strange, but what happened next was stranger still. I was a poet, yes, a poet. My English didn't exist. I was hopeless in school. Even my English teacher said I would never amount to anything. Then I said this poem out loud. Wow, I thought, that's nice, so I phoned my daughter-in-law, Kirsty, first thing in the morning. "Listen to this." So I told her the poem over the phone.

When I finished, she replied, "Derrick, I just had an electric shock run right down my back to the bottom of my feet."

She was the first person to hear *Moments*, the poem. Little did I know it would go to so many different countries. A very good friend of mine, John Young, remarked to me that *Moments* didn't belong to me. I was a little bit startled. No one messed with him in an argument. I just looked at him. He said, "It belongs to everyone." What a compliment, especially from my friend.

After all's said and done, I wasn't going to do any more, just words in my mind. The strangest thing about this poem is when I say it to certain people, they get emotional. Yet I feel something is missing… my wife.

Moments

I captured a moment, a moment in time.
I asked for no payment for the moment was mine.
I held it so tightly and wanted to stay
But I slowly released and it faded away.
So try as you may to hold on you see
You can't keep a moment that wants to be free.

Daffodils

For the next few months I went a bit crazy. Everyone I talked to, I couldn't help telling them about my experience and about the poem, *Moments*. Looking back, I must have come across a little bit strange. Yet I had this feeling something was not right with me. I found myself trying hard not to talk about poetry. I did think I was having some kind of breakdown.

The following year I decided to drive to a place called Abergavenny. Pulling over to park in a layby on the Hereford road, I was looking for a little solitude. Climbing over the stile, I followed the footpath, staying close to the edge of the field. Just about halfway up, I came upon a large stone, a place to sit, take in the view, relax.

My thoughts then seemed to run away with me. Then, as I looked upon this hill, close by there were these daffodils standing so proud. Then a breeze so gentle came and passed straight through them. It was like music. I actually could see words dancing in front of my eyes. I was witnessing this interaction going on with the breeze and daffodils. Then I realised I was having some kind of unusual experience. Another poem was going to be born. Wow, I could hear it for the first time… daffodils dancing in a gentle breeze and seem to kiss. Before I turned around to walk back to the car, another poem was born in my mind. Over and over someone was saying words to me. Getting into the car, driving away, voices, voices. I shouted as loud as I could to clear my head. I needed to see my doctor. Besides, there was something else going on. I would bring it up with him. I hoped he didn't think I was having some kind of breakdown. Then, as I drove away, I realised I had a new poem: *Daffodils.*

Daffodils

Daffodils dancing in a gentle breeze
And they seem to kiss.
Oh! What tenderness I see in this.
And as they sway and caress,
Their golden colours are expressed.
Oh! What love I see in these
While dancing in that gentle breeze.

Reminisce

The following week after *Daffodils* turned up, I decided to make an appointment to see the doctor. On Wednesday I phoned the surgery. I was offered one on Friday, eleven-thirty. Surprising how quickly two days went by.

Waiting for my name to be called in the waiting room. "Mr Mapps, you can go in now."

Feeling a little bit nervous, I knocked on his door.

"Come in."

I entered and the doctor said, "Sit down, Derrick, what can I do for you today?"

"I am having a problem, Doctor," I explained. So I started by saying about the poetry and straight away I recited *Moments*.

"That's nice, Derrick."

Before he could sit back in his chair I was saying another poem, *Daffodils*.

"That's lovely."

"Well, that's the problem, Doctor." I told him about my dream and the encounter I had.

"I will give you something to relax you, a very small dose of diazepam." He started to write out the prescription.

Plucking the courage up I said, “There is something else.”

“What’s that?” he remarked.

“Every time I look in the mirror, I don’t know who I am looking at.”

He stopped. “Derrick, you need counselling. I will refer you. They will most probably send you a letter to phone them.”

“Thank you. I will be honest, I thought it was a bit odd, Doctor.”

“Let’s get it sorted,” he replied.

With that in mind I said thank you and left. On arriving home, there were two girls waiting outside my house.

“Hello, Derrick,” they both remarked. They were the two girls who visited my wife when she was seriously ill. They were both on mission representing the Mormon Church. “We were wondering would you like to come next Thursday to a talk in Cardiff? An astronaut is speaking. By the way, there is something else, we will both be going back home soon. We will tell you when.”

I was picked up the following Thursday and enjoyed the talk. They introduced me to a lady whose husband had died of the same disease as my wife, M.N.D. I gave my phone number to her and the following week she called. After a while talking on the phone, she said, “Would you like to meet for dinner?” and I agreed.

So the following week I arrived by train. She picked me up from Cardiff railway station. Lovely woman; we talked, walked and cried. We kept in touch and eventually she moved to London to work in the Mormon temple.

On the way home on the train I could feel a sensation coming over me again as I looked out at the scenery. Another poem was born. Strangely enough, out of all the poetry, *Reminisce* is the shortest, yet in life it's the longest.

Reminisce

We met and said hello
Talked and then we strolled
We reminisced and sighed
Recalled our loved ones that had died
We sat down and we cried
We walked back and said goodbye.

Tree of Dreams

Later on in the year I had a visit from the two Mormon missionaries informing me they would be both going back. It was very moving; they both started to cry when we talked about Janet. "We will never forget her and you."

"Please call before you go back. I am going to get you something."

"We will," they replied.

What can I get them, I thought. One girl from Canada was going back hoping to become a chef. So I give her Janet's Welsh bakestone, a very heavy object. She liked the Welsh cakes. The other girl also going back, she was getting married. I bought her a set of tea towels, a reminder of Wales. If this book becomes a little successful and you are reading this, it's me…

The day came for our goodbyes. I gave them the items, they blessed me and left.

Not long after I had a letter concerning the counselling, asking me to phone and make an appointment. I made the arrangements and went along to a wonderful lady. I told her how I was feeling and wondered was it normal not to recognise yourself. I had about nine sessions and eventually I said, "I am feeling better. It is something I must come to terms with." I explained the dream, the encounter the poetry. I had a lot on my mind.

My daughter was expecting in November. Not long before the day came when my daughter was taken into hospital. I found myself driving up to Abergavenny hospital. My thoughts were everywhere, words going on in my head; trying hard to take no notice of them. It felt like people were queuing up to say lines of poetry. I arrived at the maternity ward. I talked to my daughter.

"Dad," she said, "I am okay, go home."

I could understand. I only wished her mother was with her. "Are you sure?"

"Yes, go, Dad."

Walking down the hallway I sensed this feeling, an unbelievable calmness. As I got into the car I looked straight ahead; there stood this beautiful tree. I just couldn't take my eyes off it. Then here came these words… thoughts are real or so it seems while sitting under the tree of dreams. It was back. Took tablets, had counselling. I thought I was doing okay, ignoring voices. Yet this poem turned out to be something else, the only poem that's a book in itself. Better than all the poetry you will read as you navigate through this book.

My daughter had a little girl called Chloe.

The Tree of Dreams

Thoughts are real, or so it seems
While sitting under the tree of dreams,
A place where your heart is free
And your soul can wander in and out of
reality
And certain dreams that come to mind
Quickly fade as if going blind
And then a dream that makes you feel
Where you are is so real, or so it seems
While sitting under the tree of dreams.

Places

Thoughts are real or so it seems while sitting under the tree of dreams. Over and over again this poem cried out to me. Not like any other one, this was special. I saw people, a family, in this poem; it was magical. It put right what was wrong. There was a special place. Like me, you will find out.

The tablets seemed to be helping. Also my daughter had given birth. I worried about her. She had gone back home to London. She works on the ambulances, and before that she was a paramedic in the army, which doesn't count in civilian life.

The following Saturday I visited my friend, Michael, on his farm. I always felt relaxed there. It had an ambiance all of its own.

"How are you, my good friend?" he asked. "Any more poetry?"

"Yes," I replied. "Let's have a walk around the farm."

He liked this. I did also. "Go on, tell me what's new."

"I have a new poem," I explained to him.

"Go on, tell me."

"This one poem is unusual. It's not only a poem, it's a book," I explained. So I then said the opening lines to *The Tree of Dreams*.

"I like that," he replied.

"I don't think any more will come," I replied.

"It will, Derrick, don't you worry."

I also said to him about the book. "I can see people, it's like watching a film over and over. There is something just not right."

It was always nice to visit. I felt recharged.

Over the months to come I managed to keep myself busy. The following year me and my brother, Morris, were in a place called Llanvapley, the other side of a mountain called the Skirrid, looking up. I could hear the softest sounding words. Places where you go senses overflow. Paths lead the way to where views take your breath away. Look out, it was on the march again. I like that, I thought to myself.

I told my brother. He looked at me like only a brother could, wondering should he take me to hospital, joking.

"Yes," he said, "I like it," with a smile. What a friend I have in him. We both had a love for metal detecting, him more than me. Find anything with a history about it, like a Roman coin. You would find him in the library in Cwmbran doing his research. Kings, queens of this country, he would get the information about them. I only wished he could get the book that could describe what was happening to me. He did once say to me, "Can I have the first written poem on all what I do." I did try to write them out for him. He keeps saying, "You will be famous one day." He honours me by his words.

Before we left the farm by Llanvapley, a new poem was born: *Places.*

Places

Places where they go
Where senses overflow
Paths that lead the way
To where views take your breath away

Mountain streams that whisper,
Wind that screams
Walks that feed your soul
And thoughts that turn to dreams.

Snowdrops

Places. Places. I like the line 'Mountain streams that whisper'. Have you ever sat down and listened to Canon in D Major composed by Johann Pachelbel? The softest sound in music. Yet a raindrop can turn a mountain stream into a raging river. That sounded like the applause Jonas Kaufmann received performing at the Albert Hall.

It had been just over a year and I hadn't visited my friend, Michael. All the farms were closed because of the foot and mouth outbreak and in all that time, only one line to *The Tree of Dreams* had come to be. I had been trying hard not to listen to the voices, the reason being because I saw all the characters crying out to me for them to come alive, calling, shouting, "You must write this book on us, *The Tree of Dreams*." I must be honest, the story is absolutely amazing. Nearly every night when I put my head to the pillow, it was like watching a film. I was not a writer or a poet, I was a vessel being used. Dousing is looking for ley lines, a change in the energy field. Yet I didn't find words, they found me. I needed to learn to relax and not treat the pen like a sword.

Not long after Christmas, late February, I visited a place called Maypole just outside Monmouth with my brother, Morris, and my dear friend, Richard Johns, a fantastic metal detectorist who actually went on to find one of the best medieval hoards of silver coins in the country. I promised I would mention him. Okay, that's done. There was this church with a mass of snowdrops everywhere you looked. Here goes, another one was on its way. It was a strange sensation.

As white as snow upon the ground they bow their heads as if to frown. They look so sad to me. And bitter winds will blow. *Snowdrops* was another one, born like music. I could see the notes in words, like I felt when I encountered daffodils, one of the strangest sensations and it will come up again in other chapters.

Snowdrops

As white as snow upon the ground

They bow their heads as if to frown

And bitter winds may blow

Yet strength in numbers they will show

So sad and lonely they seem to be

Yet such a flower holds the key

That others can go in

Through the gateway into spring

Yet they must stay within.

A Quest for Love

One of my favourite poems, *Snowdrops*. They alone have been entrusted with a key to open up the gateway into spring, yet they must stay. When I looked at them I saw angels' tears.

The following months to come, I was asked to go to Germany with my son, Stuart, who is in the army. Never been out of the country. Why not, I thought, it's an adventure.

On getting to Dover to cross the Channel, we were talking and suddenly I said, "There is a place within your heart where love exists, and shall I find it with a kiss," just like that.

"Dad," he said, "if you say that to any woman you would win her heart."

We both laughed. Little did I know I would be saying that to someone.

I enjoyed my trip to Germany. On one occasion, Stuart was going to work and asked me to get some washing powder. I went to the shop for washing powder and after walking around for about twenty minutes I went to the till. I can't speak German. I came out with apples. Don't laugh, it's not funny. It is.

I had such a lot of time to myself, I visited different parts of the local town looking at the old buildings. Then I had two children standing in front of me. "When are you going bring us alive?" *The Tree of Dreams* called out. They were so real to me. I will bring them alive in this world one day. First, I must complete this book.

I visited Germany on different occasions. On the last one I decided to move house, to sell, go somewhere else. Getting home I put my house up for sale and also joined a local choir, two crazy things I did, and moved.

Relaxing one evening after choir practice, the words to the poem, *Quest for Love*, came. Don't forget I had not written a poem down, they were all in my head. I had decorated my house out lovely, yet it was not a home, just a house.

One day, walking upstairs, I said out loud, "God, why can't I meet someone nice?" Little did I know the wheels of fate, call it what you may, he turned them. What can I say, I have encountered him and will again. And what kiss would it be that gives your love to me. It was like that, a flash, the words are in the poem, they are home and are not going anywhere.

A Quest for Love

There is a place within your heart

Where love exists

And shall I find it with a kiss

And what kiss would it be

That gives your love to me

Soft and gentle

And so intense

That leaves my heart in suspense

Or tender and sweet and so divine

That gives your heart to mine.

My Wife

The quest for love turned out to be just that. Little did I know when I asked God why can't I meet someone nice…

I hadn't visited my very good friend, Violet, in two weeks. I knocked her door. She answered. "Where have you been?" she enquired.

"Why, Violet?" I replied. Sat down just like a school teacher, I thought I had done something wrong.

She held my hand. "Derrick, I have something to tell you." The suspense. Then she smiled. "Derrick, I have told you before about my daughter. She was here two weeks ago and I told her about you. She gave me this telephone number on an envelope. Phone her, you have nothing to lose. I said you like poetry and that you're a nice man. It's up to you."

In the evening I plucked the courage up to phone. "Hello," I said, "my name is Derrick."

"My name is Trudy," came back the reply.

After about two hours of talking, we arranged that I would visit her home on the Tuesday coming, the last Tuesday in April. Eight-thirty I had choir practice. I stayed for the first hour, then gave my apologies and left.

Arriving outside the house I knocked the door. Nervous, yes, I was. It opened; there in front of me was this most beautiful woman.

"Hello, come in."

We talked for about three hours and then I arranged to take her out on Thursday to Tintern. On getting out of the car, she came around and held my hand to go into the restaurant. Just before we started our meal, it went so dark and then a lightning flash, then a crack of thunder; some kind of blessings on us. We were the only two in the place. We didn't stay too long, she had work in the morning.

On dropping her off, I remarked, "See you next week."

"Okay," she replied.

As soon as I was in my house, the phone rang.

"Hello. It's me, Trudy. There's a spider in my bath.

Back in the car I went over and it was only a little spider. She did not like spiders. We arranged to see each other the next day.

I took her for a drive in the country then later in the evening I dropped her off and said, "See you next Thursday."

"Okay." She got out of the car. I turned around and passed her, no wave, nothing just her head down.

I phoned as soon as I was home. "What's wrong?" I asked.

“Well,” she said, “if we are going out with each other, we go out all the time, if I am your girlfriend, are you my boyfriend?” she asked.

“Yes, I am.” My heart was singing. All I could see were her eyes. Golden. Then it started: poetry. Eyes that shine like the golden sun.

Not long after this we spent as much time with each other as we could. My heart was so contented it would cry. And the kiss… A kiss that makes you feel that life has just begun. Poetry was being born again.

We decided to live together. I think I wasn’t involved in that decision. Also that we must get married. So I sold my house and went to live with my love. With that *My Wife* was born.

My Wife

Eyes that shine
Like the morning sun,
A kiss that makes you feel
That life has just begun.
A touch that makes your heart sing,
A smile that's everything.
O what special gift I have in my life,
For you to say 'I do', to hold my hand
And walk with me, for you to be
My wife.

My Lord

My Lord found a pathway to my heart. and led love back to me. I recited this to Reverend David Bird after church on Sunday. This poem in its frame is still on show in the entrance to the church to this day. Then he arranged to visit my house on Wednesday. He then he explained to me he was doing a church fete and wanted to do an anthology of my poems. He would like my permission. Only one answer and she was standing right next to me with a smile. After we had eaten the cakes my wife, Trudy, had provided, she answered for me: yes. I looked at her; I couldn't believe how blessed I was to have her in my life. She was so proud and excited about David having the poetry for the church fete. Then she told me she was officially my manager. Her next mission was getting in touch with local craft fairs.

In the meantime, we went to the Albert Hall in London which gave Trudy the chance to dress up. No poetry could describe how beautiful she looked that night. some of the men on the bus called her Trudy Scrumptious; I will treasure that memory. When we come back, David phoned to tell us all the booklets he printed had sold out. People we met later on who had bought the booklets would say how they enjoyed reading them. I must say Trudy absolutely loved the poem *My Lord.*

On one occasion we decided to go to Hay on Wye for the world renowned book festival. We turned up at the tented village and on arrival Trudy went to the reception and told the lady, "My husband is a poet and has come to recite."

The lady went away, came back and said, "He is not booked in."

"But he is a poet," she remarked.

"Sorry, I can't do anything. Next year book him in."

They both laughed.

"We will go on to streets of Hay on Wye," was her order to me. I just remember I didn't have a say in it and I loved it. Off we went. I couldn't stop laughing.

We did well on the street. We set up a table, then people from Philadelphia, America came to our table and bought poems. "Why aren't you down there?" was their question.

"Down where?" I replied.

"The tented village."

My wife explained to them the reason why we weren't allowed.

Then a newly married couple from Ireland started to read the poetry on the table. The husband then wanted me to recite *My Wife* to his wife.

"No," I said, "it's your wife, your voice, you say it so differently." The first time I heard someone say you can't say a poem like the poet himself. I still didn't recite it. What a lovely couple; they bought the poem. God bless them.

People from Italy, France, it was going well. Then came the rain. Yet Trudy was going around giving the *My Lord* poem in bookmark form away, saying to me it was her mission to evangelise. It's surprising how many *My Lord* bookmarks are in people's bibles, all down to her. People took to her. She loved it. What a woman; what a mission. That's my wife. She is something else.

The following year our granddaughters, Livvie and Chloe came with us. We didn't book in to the tented village. We liked the atmosphere of the street. Turned up outside a hairdresser shop and after a while Trudy got pasties for us all. As we were eating a lady came out of the shop and told us to move off. We were not outside her door. Trudy looked at me and Livvie and went in. Mind you, the streets were packed. Out she came and started to eat her pasty. Me and Livvie looked at each other. Suddenly a police car pulled up and the policeman entered the shop. Out he came, looked at me, a big smile on his face. "Please," he said to me, "go across to the other side of the street."

I couldn't believe a police car would come out. What did she say? was going through our minds. Anyway, we go across the street and the police officer thanked me with a big smile on his face. Trudy never ever told us what she said. Me and Livvie always laugh about it. We continued to go to the Brecon craft fair, meeting so many lovely people from all over the country and that's a blessing in itself.

Autumn is coming… I stand in wonder at what I see…

My Lord

My Lord found a pathway

To my heart

And led love back to me

For my heart was lost

And on its own.

In that darkness I could not see,

He held my hand and led me out

And gave love back to me.

Destiny

Destiny held my heart and led my love to thee. If destiny exists then it must hide itself amongst the stars. Are we to search for it or make a wish? I always tried to imagine what she looked like. Then I looked at Trudy and realized I was looking at her. Your destiny is in the eyes of the person who loves you. Your journey starts with holding her hand.

One thing I will say to you, yes, you:

Slow everything down. Make that kiss last a little longer; that romantic evening—throw the clock away. Life will speed up; it's your job to slow it down. You will understand me one day. Perhaps you are already at that day. When you are looking back and wishing once again, don't bet me on what you're thinking, because you will lose. Don't forget, I sat on your chair once. I believe I am having a love affair with this poem. I am being unfaithful to my wife with words, because the depth of love I am expressing, like the soft caress of one's heart. Don't forget a raindrop can fill an ocean. and a teardrop can too. So don't cry.

The person who designed my poems asked me had I written another poem. *Destiny*, I replied out of the blue. I wasn't even thinking of poetry. It was if someone else answered the question. Then he left it up to me to compose the poem. I honestly thought there were two people writing this. The last lines in this poem came first and will come up again in another poem that's very true, for no river runs as fast, or seas shall be so deep. So I rest my case for destiny, as we all have a path in our lives. Yet mine keeps occurring. For some reason I have been given a gift to hear it first. A true poet writes poetry to himself. Sometimes it feels like a river in flood. Or a breeze so gentle it whispers to your heart. And you are the only person who can hear them. It's not how far a teardrop falls from your eyes. It's the feeling that releases them. Heartache or happiness, it's still a tear. Which one would you like to release? Remember you can't know happiness, until you have known sadness.

Life is so beautiful. Stop, look, it's all around: *Destiny*.

Destiny

Destiny held my heart
And led my love to thee
No poet can express in words
All you mean to me
Thoughts of love and desire
Are deep within my soul
Caress my heart and inspire
To say the words I am told
For no river runs as fast
Or seas shall be so deep
In fact it is the mystery
My heart will have to keep

Home

A very special poem to me, *My Wife*. If you love your wife like these words you are doing well…

One evening, coming home from choir practice, I came in through the front door. "Stay there," she called out. "Don't come in."

I was thinking, what's wrong.

"Close your eyes." She opened the door to the lounge. "Turn right," she said. "Open your eyes."

Looking down on the table, all the poems I had told her, she wrote them down and put them on the laptop, designing all night and putting them all in frames.

My reaction to seeing them for the first time in writing: "Wow, that's really nice, Tuds." That was her mother's special name for her. I just done the same.

"Right," she said, "we are going to Tintern Abbey on Sunday to sell them."

Looking at her, I had no chance. I just followed and I loved it.

There outside the abbey was a pub called The Anchor. I went in and asked to see the landlord. I asked him for permission to come in and put the table up on the green.

"No trouble," he replied.

We were there for two hours. People looked, talked, didn't buy. Anyway, it's nice to converse with them. Just then a number of motorcycles come driving down. I looked: Hells Angels. The lead biker had a funny helmet on and I believe it was his wife on the back. They all got off the bikes and walked straight to the table, following the woman who was on the first bike. She said hello to Trudy, then looked and picked up one to read.

The one with the basin-shaped helmet, her husband was standing right up close to me and commented, "I don't like poetry."

Me, being confident, replied, "I don't too."

He looked down and started reading a poem, then he said, "I will buy that one."

I said, "You're a big softy."

He smiled and picked up *My Wife*. The lady bought *Daffodils,* our first. Trudy held my hand, kissed me, saying, "I told you so."

I never will forget that day. Everything was falling in place. Trudy's best friend invited us to her brother's birthday party. I met up with someone who would always be special to me. Obviously I started talking about poetry, telling him about them.

"What's your address and phone number? I will call down in the week and see you. I have some ideas."

Wednesday came, knock on the door, there was Robert. We talked. I listened because he talked about computers; I hadn't a clue. He took *Moments* with him.

The following Saturday we were up Brecon craft fair. Halfway through Robert turned up with *Moments;* he had designed it. I put it on the centre of the table and it went straight away. After that he said he would design all the poems.

In the following weeks we set off to Prague with the choir. It was a very picturesque place yet so cold and expensive. Yet something happened there again. The choir was just about to sing in the second half when this poem came to me. After it was finished Trudy asked me why I was smiling.

I said, "I was singing and a poem was coming into life once again."

She said, "I told you you didn't have go to a special place for poetry to find you."

There is a place called home where valleys fill your heart and mountains feed your soul. *Home* was born.

Home

There is a place I call home
Where valleys fill your heart
Mountains feed your soul
Where songs carry on the wind
Angels listen when choirs sing
Where passion flows like rivers run
Hills that kiss the morning sun
Where views can captivate your eyes
Mountains seem to hold the sky
There in that place my heart belongs
And if I should go away from home
Then I hope my dreams carry my soul
And take my heart back home again.

Poppies

There was a line missing in the *Home* poem: where songs carry on the wind.

Angels listen when choirs sing. I think this is a welsh poem. No, I don't think, I know. Where else would an angel stop to hear a choir? A Welsh choir.

"Okay, Mr Mapps, we are finished." Coming out of the CT scan, problem with my thyroid. "Did you enjoy the music?"

"What music?"

"You had the headphones on."

"I wasn't listening to it, I was hearing poetry."

She looked at me. "Don't be silly."

"No," I said, "honest."

"Go on, then tell me the poem."

I recited *Moments.*

"That's lovely," she replied. "Stay there, I am going to get the superintendent."

Out the two came. "Go on," she said, "tell her the poem."

I recited *Moments* again and they both looked at me.

The superintendent said, "Mr Mapps, our colleague died. She was only thirty-four, a radiologist. Please may we have the poem? We will pay you."

"No, it's okay," I replied.

"How much?" they insisted.

"Ten pounds," I replied. "It will go to good works," I said.

My daughter was waiting outside and I told her.

"Dad, we will go home and get it, take it straight back up."

"That's fine with me." I couldn't get over it, one of my poems would be on the wall in Abergavenny Nevill Hall Hospital.

On arriving home, I went straight upstairs, opened the cupboard and put *Moments* in the bag. It went a bit strange again. A voice said put *Snowdrops* in. That went in the bag and I turned to go again, then the voice said put *Daffodils* in. Back downstairs, headed back to Abergavenny to the CT's reception suite. I explained to the lady that I had something for the superintendent. She then called the nurse who attended me when I was in the CT scan room. Up she came. I showed her the *Moments* poem.

"That's lovely, Mr Mapps. Here is your ten pounds."

"By the way," I said to her, "look at this," and showed her *Snowdrops*.

She read it and started crying. She called the superintendent who read it and she started crying. I was standing there looking at the two women crying. They said, “It was her favourite flower. That’s all she would go on about, snowdrops, snowdrops it would drive us crazy.

The two poems are on the wall in that hospital. Unbelievably true. I went out tell my daughter and we went downstairs, raining terrible outside.

“Have a cup of tea, Dad,” she remarked. “There’s a café in Neville hall. Get a seat, Dad.”

It looked quite full. There was a lady sitting up the top end. “Are these. two seats spare?” I asked.

“Yes,” she replied.

“Terrible day out,” I said.

“Yes, it is,” she replied, then she said to me, “They told me my cancer has come back.”

I didn’t know what to say. I touched her hand saying, “You will be okay, my love.” Straight away I changed the subject to the weather. “Terrible out.”

“Yes,” she replied.

“Where are you from?”

“Merthyr.”

I asked her what did she like doing.

“Gardening, I love my garden.”

Here it came. “What’s your favourite flower?”

She said it like this: “My favourite flower ever is daffodils.

My daughter looked at me.

As we finished our tea, I said, “I am going now.”

“Goodbye,” she said.

I got the poem out of my bag, put it upside down on the table. "Goodbye. This is yours. Look at it when I have gone."

Strange, you might think, but it's so true.

Going back home, my thoughts were everywhere.

About a week later, watching on the television a place called Royal Wotton Bassett. It gained its royal entitlement because of the great sadness and understanding the people showed to the soldiers returning home from Afghanistan. Suddenly poppies came to mind. I held a flower in my hand caressed it to my soul… Yet I was seeing a mother holding her son and taking him into a special field. This to me is so special, I had tears in my eyes when I first heard it; read with your heart.

Poppies

I held a flower in my hand
Caressed it to my soul
While walking in a field of gold
Then as I gently let it go

A crimson tear fell from my eye
And stained the petals so
Precious flowers now exist
In that field of gold.

Grief

Poppies. A crimson tear fell from my eye and stained the petal so I was observing families losing their loved ones, and then a poem was born. A mother taking her son into a special place, then by her crimson tears created a flower called a poppy. She must leave her son yet she will never forget him. Unbelievably I sensed her heartache. Little did I know I was going to share it to.

About four months went by. I was on tour with my wife, a trip with the choir to Cornwall. The first night there, there was a phone call in the early hours of the morning. "Hello," I said.

"It's me, Stuart."

"Yes," I said.

"Gary has died, Dad."

Then the silence. People talked to me, yet it was like being under water. The days went on. and on.

I couldn't believe it. My friend, my son who I loved dearly, had died. I couldn't accept it. The funeral came and went, yet it never ends in your heart, the ache, like your chest is going to explode. My wife was in work I was in the house walking from room to room, out to the kitchen, back in the room. I went back out to the kitchen and I called out, "God help me. I can't carry this."

Then a voice said to me, “Derrick, my son died too.” Just like that, my Lord talked to me. It was like a blanket being put over my heart and to this day it’s still in place.

Then words started to come. Grief is no friend of mine. Nobody wants him as a friend, yet he stays with you till it’s time for him to go. While that poem was going on, another was calling out to me. Like a soft whisper saying, “Don’t forget us.” *The Tree of Dream*s was back, saying, “You must write about us.” My mind could picture them, a boy and girl. Then I saw this tree, a massive tree with a wrought iron seat going right around the tree, and as it grew it had become one with the seat. Then these words came. My heart was lost… and on its own. In that darkness I could not see. What lovely words. Then I realised another poem was on its way.

Grief

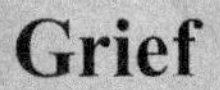

Grief is no friend of mine

Like an uninvited guest

That drinks your wine

Yet he turns to me and smiles,

How long will he stay?

As long as I feel this way.

Then I turn to him and smile.

I guess you're with me for a while.

Autumn

How can you compete with autumn? The colours are in competition with each other, to gain recognition, to win your heart. It's a gift of nature, a master painter, yet with words I will try to take up the challenge. A war, yes, for victory, and whoever loses must go into winter. It's actually one sided. I have the pen. Say nothing. Our secret.

I decided to take Trudy to Tintern Abbey for Sunday lunch at The Anchor Inn, lovely place, very friendly atmosphere. After dinner we went for a walk. Just outside at the bottom of the road leading in to the abbey shop, there was a roundabout and in the middle stood a miller's stone. I said to Trudy, "See that stone, the one with the hole in it?"

"Yes," she replied.

"Legend states that if a couple stands either side and holds hands, keys to each other's heart will be exchanged and you will get married."

Suddenly, like a fish on a hook, she tugged my hand and started to take me into the centre. I was standing there, cars going around. She said to me, "Put your hand through." I said no and she laughed. "Go on," she said.

I put my hand just inside and she grabbed it.

"How long must we stay like this?" I said.

"About a minute."

Cars were going around, people looking at us. I was so in love with this woman.

We carried on with our walk back on the pathway to a the bridge over the river Wye. On getting there we both stopped to take in the autumn colours, a painter's palette with the colours green, red, yellow and brown, running into each other; the more you looked, the more he brushed them into each other. Then as we both started to cross, I was wondering what could I say to this beautiful woman standing next to me…

"Trudy, this bridge has a name."

"What?" she remarked.

"The bridge of broken dreams," I replied. "Yet if you walk halfway across and look to your left you can make a wish."

I had no chance, like the stone. She stopped halfway across, let go of my hand and told me to walk on. Off I went.

"How long must I stay here?" she said to me.

"As long as your wish," I replied. My heart could not contain itself. Words came dancing from the trees… What gift nature gives my eyes to look upon on this glorious prize…

She caught up with me.

"What was your wish?"

"It's a secret."

I told her the lines. of a poem that had just come to me: *Autumn*.

She looked at me shaking her head, then she said to me, “You’re like Mozart. You pick your words out of the air like he picked the music notes out of the sky.” She held me and whispered, “You’re mine.”

The following week I arranged a dinner date in the Chinese restaurant in Cwmbran. I told the manager I would bring the flowers on the day for the table, and the engagement ring. I wanted him to tie the ring on her favourite pink gerbera flower, and for it to face her on the table.

Saturday night came, into the reception we entered. I enquired, “Are there any tables free?”

The manager looked at me with a smile. “I will look, sir.” We sat down and waited then he came back. “We have had a cancellation. Come this way.”

There were about twenty people seated. He took us to the table, pulled the chair out for my Trudy. We sat.

Wow, it was over. What a week, keeping it secret. She looked across the table, looked at the flowers and compared them to the other tables and just smiled. We had our starters, looking at each other talking, and there was this ring dangling right in front of her eyes. I couldn’t believe it. I looked over to the manager and his staff, all waiting. for her reaction.

“Lovely flowers, Trudy,” I said.

“Yes,” she remarked, “beautiful.”

You would not believe it unless you were there. I sort of gave up. The waiter came and took the plates away. “Are you ready to order your main course?”

“Yes.”

There was a scream so loud, love her. I was beginning to wonder would I have to tell her… She couldn’t wait to put it on her finger. Then they all started clapping, everyone was in on it. O what special gift I have in my life. A line that belongs in the *My Wife* poem.

I stand in wonder at what I see gazing at the autumn leaves. What gift nature gives my eyes. just looking at this glorious prize: *My Wife*.

Autumn

I stand in wonder at what I see
Gazing at the autumn trees
Leaves cascade with golden colours
Shades of yellow reflect the sun
Fiery reds blaze through the leaves
As they turn to chestnut brown
Gently falling to the ground
What gift nature gives my eyes
To look upon this glorious prize

Bluebells

The most peaceful place to be is a bluebell wood. This was an experience one Sunday, coming back from Monmouth down the Wye Valley as far as Tintern Abbey. My wife and I, we have one thing in common: we like to get lost in the country lanes. I turned off on to an old road. I was actually looking for a stone for our garden, something unusual, the reason being I made a promise that I that I was going to make a miniature standing stone with violets growing all around to ease her heart. She had lost her mother, Violet.

So, it had to be special.

We pulled into the layby. Getting out of the car to stretch our legs, we were confronted with a sight: a sea of blue as far into the woods as we could see, blue as blue could be. There among the flowers stood a white bluebell. I pointed it out to Trudy. She remarked that it looked so lonely.

I replied with one of my stories. "No, in fact the opposite; she is an ancient Celtic princess, and all the bluebells are guarding her until her prince returns." You must understand, she believed me. I started to think it was true. Then I said, "A kiss will release the spell and next year two white bluebells will be there."

"What do you mean, a kiss?" she asked.

I explained. "The ones who have seen her must kiss."

She looked at me and I ran around the car with her chasing me. I made sure I was caught and that day the spell was broken. All the way home I was just driving. Trudy was sleeping; she had released a princess. You couldn't make it up. I did; she believed.

The next day it started again. I kept seeing the sunlight dancing on the leaves.

About one week later we visited my sister, Moreen Lewis, who lived in a place called Llanbradach. Trudy told her about the bluebells we had seen the previous week.

"We have a beautiful bluebell wood," Moreen explained.

"Come on, let's go see," Trudy insisted.

Out to the car. I was just the chauffeur; they so liked each other. They laughed together. My sister loved her because of who she was.

When we got to Margaret's wood in Llanbradach, out of the car in no time, Trudy jumped over the gate and ran through the bluebells.

"They are so beautiful, Moreen."

All I could see was the lights in words casting shadows on the ground. A poem was being born as she stopped and sat by a tree. I could see her dreaming. A sea of blue held her eyes. Thoughts of love came rushing through my mind. I was in a bluebell poem. The unknown does exist; it's just there if you look but not with your eyes, with your heart.

Bluebells
To walk amongst the tallest trees
Speckled lights dance off the leaves
Casting shadows on the ground
Bluebells growing all around
A fallen tree lies by a stream
A place to rest and to dream
The sea of blue holds my eyes
As thoughts of love swell deep inside
So deep, moving and serene
As I looked upon that peaceful scene

Warrior

Once a fortnight I visited my good friend, Michael, who lived in Abergavenny. Saturday morning, beautiful day. On arriving he treated me to coffee and biscuits under the pergola overlooking the river Usk. In the distance. one mountain stood out to me, the Skirrid. My eyes were transfixed, my soul seemed to shiver.

Carrying a tray, Michael put it on the table. "Help yourself, Derrick."

Then I came out with this line… "O what great battle must have taken place to see the scars upon your face."

He looked at me. "Derrick, that's powerful."

I thought so myself. "There was something about that mountain," I explained. "It just exploded in my mind."

That was the first time he witnessed. the words coming out of my mouth. "I look forward to hearing it when it's finished."

"Me too," I replied.

We then turned the conversation to local Celtic and Roman history, a subject we liked, yet as we talked my eyes were drawn to this mountain. Trying to listen to my friend with the words rushing into my mind.

"Listen to this, Michael," I said, breaking our conversation. I then said this: "No history book can recall the battle that saved us all." My body was tingling.

"That's moving," he replied.

I so liked visiting Michael. It was like a spiritual uplifting to my soul.

I told him about this other poem that came to me in the week, called *Love*. The funny part about this, there are two poems on the same subject. One opens up: Love don't dwell in words. It takes flight in thought. The other one: If words could give your love to me.

"I can't wait to hear them, Derrick," he replied.

Yet I was still drawn to the mountain.

I said my goodbyes with our usual handshake and he replied like he always did, "See you in two weeks."

Getting in the car, I decided to go on the Heads of the Valley road, just for a drive, yet words were dancing about in front of me. I could see this ancient warrior standing in front of me, a scar on his face. I found out later there is a church on that mountain called St Michael's, yet I like to believe I saw Michael the angel warrior in front of me that day when I was driving.

By the time I saw my friend two weeks later, this poem was finished. I must say this poem is so powerful. You read it. Make your own mind up… *Warrior.*

Warrior

Oh what great battle must have taken place
To see the scars upon your face
Yet no history book can recall
The battle that saved us all
You lie there silent yet awake
Waiting for the day to break
When the call to arms is made
Rise the warrior from the grave
A thousand voices sang your praise
For the bravery you displayed
And the courage that was shown
Guarding the gateway to our home

Love

For some time one poem never had a name. I kept on calling it *The Skirrid Mountain* up until it was designed. Then I knew in my all heart the poem belonged to all who needed a warrior to turn up in their lives, so I told my daughter, Sarah, the name: *Warrior*. Then I waited until she sent me the picture. What a surprise, first thing in the morning it was waiting on my Messenger, what a design. I bought a frame, attached the photo, just could not stop looking at it.

My next door neighbour, who was a sergeant in the Royal Marines, would be a good judge, I thought. One day, outside my house talking to him, I said, “Look at this for me, please.” I handed the poem to him and walked away to let him look and read it.

A few minutes went by and he was still standing there. Then he turned around. Looking at me, he said, “You have something here, Derrick.”

He was the first person to buy one to give to a brigadier. Then his wife asked me for one, so she could give it to him for their anniversary. Then one morning he knocked my door. “Can I buy another one of *Warrior*?”

I couldn't say yes because it would spoil his surprise. I said to him, "I sold them, sorry."

He loved his surprise, I was told later.

While that was all going on, two different poems on love were fighting to come out. If words could give your love to me I would seek them so. Sadly it lost out to love don't dwell in words it takes flight in thought. This, out of all the poems I had recited, I just couldn't help looking in the person's eyes, as I proceeded. I got so far then tears started forming in their eyes. It was very moving. I believe one day it will be up there with one off the best love poems, the way the words call out. In this poem, you're thinking that you would be happy just to hear her voice. Or search dreams. And then you compare distance between each other by using stars. Your heart must rest if you're going to search the universe for love.

So we settled on a cruise in the Mediterranean Sea. About three months after our holiday, one evening we were talking about our adventures. Just as we were both relaxing on the settee, suddenly out came the start of another poem: What lucky person I have become I cast my lot.

"Trudy, I am sitting underneath the cross," I remarked. She looked across to me and just smiled.

About a week later she showed me a Beatrix Potter book and then explained to me, "You must do the same, chapter and then the verse. Tell people how the different poems come to you."

So if you're reading this, my wife, Trudy, was right. She would always say to me I see in words and she is so right, for every time I look at her I see… love.

Love

Love doesn't dwell in words
It takes flight in thought
So I think of you

For my love has searched a
thousand dreams
To seek solace in your heart
No distant stars
Shall be as far
As we are apart

So, I close my eyes
I visualise
You standing next to me
For my heart was broken
No words were spoken
My love reached out in vain
For words like my tear drops
I hide them in the rain

The Cross

Every journey has a beginning and it turns out mine has to end. The heart can die so many different ways, yet mine ends at the cross.

Like I have said in a previous chapter, the end of this poem came just after the first opening two lines. This is how poetry happens to me. The words appear like pictures and it feels so real to me. It's like I can see what's taken place. I actually cried a number of times as this was being composed. Not a sight to hold too long in your mind to see people gamble over a crimson robe. I am like some kind of witness as I observe it.

My son, Stuart, who was in the army, showed this poem to the chaplain. He phoned me to ask permission to do a sermon on the poem the coming Easter. I was quite moved. I said you don't need my permission to speak on the cross.

Back to the poem, the words came; once more I could hear the conversation going on above me when holding his robe, word for word.

The next time was in Barcelona. Me and my wife, Trudy, were walking up the road to the square from the harbour. There was a church halfway up, on the left.

"Let's go in," she remarked.

On entering we were treated to the most beautiful carved statues. She took the camera and off she went. I looked to my left, where there was a small side room, and at the back was the cross, in wood, beautifully carved. No words could describe my thoughts. Then, the light came through the window on one side, yet it was so dark on the other side of the room, like some kind of struggle going on between them.

That set me off again… darkness fell upon the land. held the light at bay. Just like that the words came.

Later on in the holiday we visited Rome. They say you can't see it in one day; I did, my Trudy was with me.

We eventually came home. She had a nasty cold yet she still went into work to tell her friends about her holiday. She made an appointment to see the doctor.

Everything went so fast. By Monday I had to take her to hospital and before long she was admitted to ICU. I was talking to her about this poem. "I have done everything," I said, "but it has no end."

She looked at me. "You have the ending, remember."

"What do you mean?" I asked.

She came back with this reply. Then as I turned to walk away I felt a sense of shame I asked a woman standing there did she know his name. Trudy ended the poem, *The Cross*.

My beloved wife, Trudy, it was her idea about this book. She honoured me and died the next day with these words: I LOVE YOU…

The Cross

What a lucky person I have become
I cast my lot and I have won
A crimson robe was my prize
I raised my head and heard these cries
"If you're the Christ like they say
Get down off that cross and walk away."

Then a voice said, "Let him be, he's innocent, we are guilty
A crown of thorns upon his head
He looked across and then he said
"For what you had to say, you will be in paradise with me today."

Darkness then fell upon the land
Held the light at bay
"It is finished!"
I heard him cry
He bowed his head and then he died.

As I looked upon the cross
I could not understand
Why this man asked his father to forgive me
For the marks upon his hands
Then as I turned to walk away
I felt a sense of shame
I asked a woman standing there
"Did she know his name?"

Printed in Great Britain
by Amazon